BUILDING YOUR FIRST WOODEN BOAT

BUILDING YOUR FIRST WOODEN BOAT

George W. Barnes

VAN NOSTRAND REINHOLD COMPANY
New York Cincinnati Toronto London Melbourne

Printed in the United States of America
Designed by Loudan Enterprises

Published in 1979 by Van Nostrand Reinhold Company
A division of Litton Educational Publishing, Inc.
135 West 50th Street, New York, N.Y. 10020, U.S.A.

Van Nostrand Reinhold Limited
1410 Birchmount Road
Scarborough, Ontario M1P 2E7, Canada

Van Nostrand Reinhold Australia Pty. Ltd.
17 Queen Street
Mitcham, Victoria 3132, Australia

Van Nostrand Reinhold Company Limited
Molly Millars Lane
Wokingham, Berkshire, England

16   15   14   13   12   11   10   9   8   7   6   5   4   3   2   1

Library of Congress Cataloging in Publication Data

Barnes, George W   date
Building your first wooden boat.

Includes index.
1. Skiffs—Design and construction. 2. Boat-
building. I. Title.
VM355.B37   623.82'02   79-4677
ISBN 0-442-21571-1

*Dedicated to my father, Henry,
who is pictured throughout and
who has forgotten more about
boats than I'll ever know.*

Contents

Introduction

Why another book on building small boats? This is a logical question when you consider the number of boating magazines currently published that each year contain small boat designs, the availability of plans from other sources, and the relative ease and economy with which a commercially built small boat can be obtained. The key words are "design" and "plans." Boats might have been designed and produced from plans, yet some to the older practiced eye do not even look like boats.

The construction procedures detailed in this book involve neither a design nor plans. True, the outcome is predictable, but each boat built this way will be slightly different, with its own character and personality. The building process described here has been used for a hundred or more years, and it should be recorded before the art is lost, for it is an art.

Not only does each boat have its own personality and character, but also each carries a small portion of the character and personality of the builder. Each builder imparts a slightly different approach and uses his own unique techniques, so his boat will have a particular aspect that he feels makes it just a little bit better than the "other fella's." Yet it's an endless argument as to which model is the best. This argument alone may have fostered the downeast story found in each coastal community that "John" can go into the woods with a bucksaw and axe in the fall and come out in the spring with a boat.

If you doubt that these boats have both character and personality, you have only to go to some secluded cove by a fishing village when the sun is just setting and the water is reflecting a myriad of colors. Watch and study the tethered skiffs as they move gently in the evening breeze. Sometimes they almost appear to be conversing and retelling the day's events. As the light changes and the edge of darkness approaches, only a little imagination is required to see them settling in for a night's rest. Replace these boats with those built from standardized machine-made molds or with those exhibiting the uniformity of preplanned and precut construction and the effect is lost.

The instructions given in this book will produce a boat with individuality. It will not, however, be an exact duplicate of the craft pictured. A little bit of your own life and experience will be built into her, and a new character and personality will appear on the bay when she is launched.

The uses to which a skiff can be put are myriad. More miles have probably been traveled by rowing than under power, for the advent of the outboard is really comparatively recent. For those who enjoy rowing or seek a peaceful form of exercise, what could be more satisfying than rowing a skiff you built yourself. And think of the energy conservation features.

Many boaters are attracted to gunkholing and exploring less populated areas. The shallow draft of a skiff is ideal for exploring the heads of navigable waters, picnicing, remote beachcombing, etc.—you name it and there's an application from the plain fun of just being on the water to earning a living.

The dimensions given are for a finished skiff a little over fourteen feet long and approximately four feet wide on the bottom. For family fun, including fishing, a ten horsepower outboard motor should provide sufficient power.

The dimensions can be increased proportionately if a larger work boat is needed for lobstering, commercial fishing, sea mossing and similar endeavors or be reduced to the neighborhood of ten feet in length if a tender for a larger boat is desired.

Construction Materials

The traditional building materials for a downeast skiff are white pine and red oak. Pine is used for the "skin" of the craft, while oak provides the necessary reinforcement, strength,and high density in areas of wear and impact. Only "select"-grade lumber should be used, particularly the pine to be used for the sides of the skiff. This pine should be sound, free of knots, fully seasoned, and of the highest quality. A few small knots, as long as they are not loose or large enough to be easily dislodged, will do no harm.

In some areas, both pine and oak can be obtained from mills that specialize in ship lumber and timber. Along the coast, some saw mills retain and season high-quality pine for boat building whenever they find some, but good quality white pine is becoming more difficult to find as time goes on. It will be well to initiate a search for suitable pine well in advance of your planned construction, since the search may take time. Oak should not be difficult to locate in areas where boat building and supporting saw mills prevail but may not be readily available from lumber outlets specializing in ordinary building materials. It may be possible, however, to locate the necessary lumber in well-stocked commercial lumberyards, but if this source of supply is used, care must be taken to ensure that the lumber is of a grade adequate for marine use.

Caulking cotton, seam compound, and bedding compound can be obtained from most ship chandlers or marine hardware stores. Recently, twisted caulking cotton has been in short supply; in some areas it has disappeared from the market. If twisted cotton cannot be found, untwisted may be used, but the latter is less convenient than twisted cotton for a number of the steps involved in skiff construction.

Ferrous nails, screws, and bolts should all be hot-dip galvanized, especially if the skiff is to be used in salt water. Cadmium-plated fastenings should be avoided, but nonferrous fastenings, though expensive, are excellent. Even in fresh water, the life of the skiff will be extended considerably if hot-dip galvanized or nonferrous fastenings are used.

With the ever-increasing use of fiberglass in boat construction, clench nails have become almost nonexistent. Skookum Fastening Company (West 1801 Eleventh Avenue, Spokane, Washington 99204) has started producing these nails in a pattern slightly different from the traditional, but they are very acceptable. Unless you are lucky enough to find a boatyard or marine hardware company that still has some clench nails available, Skookum is apparently the only source of supply, since an intensive search has revealed no other manufacturers. Substitute fastenings can be used, but these clench nails can draw two pieces of wood together better than any other fastening method. If clench nails prove to be unavailable, copper rivets and burrs can be used with good results. A special tool designed for the size of the burr used will have to be obtained. Unlike clench nailing, which can be done by one person, rivetting requires two people working together.

About paint: There are a number of different types of marine antifouling paint now on the market, ranging from the old tried-and-true copper paint to some of the more recent developments, such as the hard-surface antifouling paints. All of these paints contain various metals to retard the growth of marine vegetation, the attachment of barnacles, and the entrance of marine borers. If the skiff is to be used only in fresh water, a type of bottom paint specially formulated for fresh water may be used.

A variety of formulas will also be found in marine enamels for topsides use. There are now dozens of above-water paints for this purpose. One of the old standbys is ship-and-deck enamel, which is produced by most of the major paint manufacturers. I have had excellent results with both marine acrylic enamels and good quality porch and floor enamels, but no matter the paint used, repainting will be necessary each spring.

The materials list that follows is for a skiff approximately 14 feet long. If a larger or smaller boat is desired, the list may be easily modified accordingly.

Construction Materials

2	13/16″ x 14″ minimum x 16′ pine (bottom of sides)
2	13/16″ x 12″ x 16′ pine (top of sides)
1	13/16″ x 8″ x 16′ pine (seats)
1	13/16″ x 12″ x 6′ pine (stern seat)
100	board feet select pine 13/16″ x 6″ wide (bottom)
2	3″ x 3″ x 4′ oak (stem and false stem)
1	1″ x 10″ x 12′ oak (transom)
3	1″ x 6″ x 16′ oak (inner and outer bottom strip and side strips)
1	1″ x 6″ x 16′ oak or pine (scrub strips for gunnels)
1	1″ x 6″ x 16′ oak (cleats for side and stern)
1	1″ x 12″ x 3′ oak (center cleat for stern board or transom)
1	2″ x 12″ x 2′ oak (stern knee)
1	lb. twisted caulking cotton
1	qt. marine seam compound
1	small can bedding compound, such as Bedlast
3	lbs. 6-penny galvanized nails
4	lbs. 8-penny galvanized nails
1	box 1½″ No. 12 galvanized screws
50	1¼″ No. 10 galvanized screws
2	lbs. 1⅛″ clench nails or substitute
1	pair hot-dip galvanized Davis oarlocks
10	¼″ x 3″ hot-dip galvanized carriage bolts with flat washers
2	qts. antifouling marine bottom paint
1	gal. marine enamel

Prices will, of course, vary from area to area depending upon available discounts, volume of trade, etc., so it is impossible to quote firm prices here. In our locality the above materials will currently cost in the neighborhood of $250 to $300. If confronted with a tight budget, the best suggestion is to carefully price the entire material listing at the sources of supply before making any purchases.

Tools and Equipment 2.

There is, of course, no standard set of tools for building a skiff, any more than there is for building a house, a barn, or anything else made of lumber. The tools and equipment listed here will provide a more than adequate assortment to produce a boat of excellent quality with a good appearance. Some of the power tools listed are expensive and probably should not be purchased for one project. But don't let the lack of power tools prevent you from building a skiff if you really want one. There have probably been more small boats built before power tools were available than since. Power tools are a tremendous aid and time saver, but their use is not mandatory or necessary. If you feel you must use power tools but feel you can't afford them, tool rental businesses should not be overlooked as a potential source. If tools are rented, it will be well to arrange things so the power tool work can be done at one time, since rentals can be expensive, too. Another alternative is to take "special cuts" to a professional woodworking shop for custom cutting. Usually a shop of this nature can be found nearby.

Hand Tools

Bit brace
Block plane
C-clamps (assortment of 4″ to 6″—at least eight)
Carpenter's bevel
Carpenter's hammer
Carpenter's square
Caulking iron
Caulking roller
Chisels (assorted sizes, up to 2″)
Clenching iron (any heavy iron with a flat surface)
Drawshave
Hand crosscut saw
Hand rip saw
Nail set (large, with ¼″ face)
Paint brushes
Scraper*
Screwdriver for bit brace
Set of wood bits
Smoothing plane
Spokeshave (flat)
Try square
Twist drills
Wrenches

Power Tools

Band Saw
Drill (¼″ or ⅜″)
Power hand saw
Table saw or radial-arm saw

Miscellaneous

Carpenter's horses (four to six)
Straightedge

*Directions for making a homemade scraper can be found in *Making Bamboo Rods* by George W. Barnes (Winchester Press, New York).

3

Preliminaries

To begin construction, the lumber for the two bottom sideboards or side planks, and the two top sideboards are paired, and each pair is nailed together temporarily on carpenter horses (figures 3-1 and 3-2). The two bottom sideboards are in their final relative position; in other words, the flat contact surface between the two boards will become the inside of the skiff. Due to the lapped joint of the sideboards, which will be described later, the reverse is true of the top sideboards; the outside surfaces of these boards will become the inside of the skiff.

Once temporarily assembled, the two pairs of boards are brought in contact edge to edge, as shown by the dotted line in figure 3-2. To insure that the top and bottom boards will fit together exactly,two or three cuts with a power hand saw are made down the entire length of the joint between the boards (figure 3-3). In doing this, care should be taken to keep the saw blade running in the joint area. It is not at all essential that this cut line be exactly straight, but it is imperative that the two pairs of boards match perfectly along their entire length.

Some sources of supply may provide boards that are not edged in order to gain maximum widths. When this type of pine board is used, it is not necessary to "square" the boards, since the joint between the top and bottom boards does not have to be parallel with the skiff bottom. Improved dimensions, height, and sheer may result from using a tapered bottom sideboard. The drawings show "squared" sideboards, but in the photographs, tapered boards are being used.

If a very high-sided skiff is planned, three sideboards with two lapped joints may be required. When this approach is taken, the center sideboard should be "squared," and each side should be jointed so that the edges remain parallel the entire length of the center sideboard.

3-1. *The top and bottom sideboards or planks nailed together in pairs, ready for cutting.*

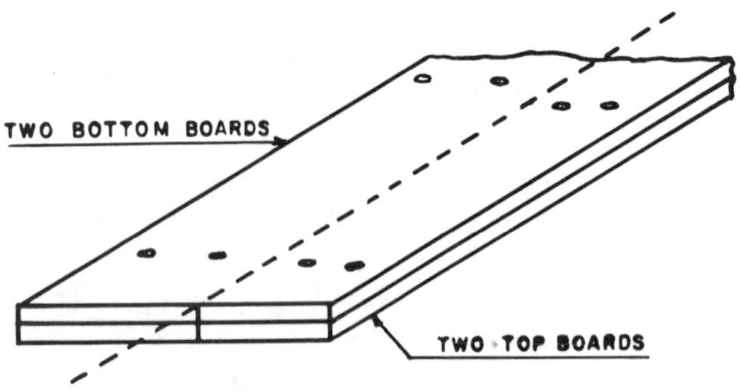

3-2. *The paired-up boards nailed together and placed edge-to-edge. A saw cut along the joint will insure a perfect match.*

3-3. *Trimming the joint between the sideboard pairs with a power saw to insure that the top and bottom boards will fit together exactly.*

As soon as the saw cuts are completed and a perfect match is attained, the boards are clamped at one or two points using C-clamps and are turned on edge to plane the saw cuts just completed (figure 3-4). The C-clamps simply insure that the boards will not sag in the middle in areas where they are not nailed together.

Once both pairs of boards have been planed along the saw cuts, they are again placed flat on the saw horses, and the boards are marked for additional cutting. A typical layout for these cuts is shown in figure 3-5. The dimensions given will produce a skiff somewhat over 14 feet long, of good proportions. The beauty of this type of skiff construction is that at this point in the building process, size adjustments can be made to suit the individual builder. If a higher-sided skiff is desired, it is only necessary to use a wider pair of top boards to increase the overall height of the sides. If less rake to the bow is desired, it is only necessary to increase the angle shown. Similarly, if a squarer stern is desired, the angle shown can be increased. And, if more sheer is desired, the 2-inch sheer shown in figure 3-5 can also be increased.

3-4. A pair of sideboards clamped together and being finish-planed along their edges. Note the scrap lumber used to protect the horse when making saw cuts.

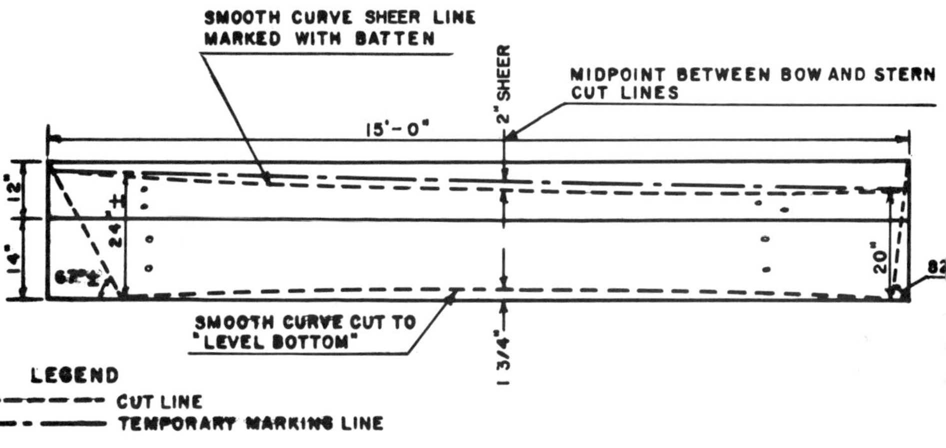

3-5. Layout for the basic sideboard cuts.

The 1¾-inch cut shown on the pair of bottom sideboards will give the skiff a relatively flat bottom when the sides are bent into their final position. In years gone by, when power was provided only by oars, many skiff builders did not give their skiffs flat bottoms. Rather, they gave them rounded bottoms (fore and aft) that would leave less of the skiff's bottom in contact with the water and therefore provide easier rowing. Most skiffs are now propelled by outboard motors, and a flat bottom does have the advantage of increasing contact with the water and thus stability.

The first marks made in the boards are the cut lines for the angles of the bow and the stern (figure 3-6). Using a long straight-edge, a straight line is then struck from bow to stern; in essence, the height of both the bow and the stern is determined by the intersection of this line with the bow and stern lines. It is well to remember at this point, however, that the lap joint used in the construction of the sides will reduce this height about 1¼ inches.

The 2-inch sheer as depicted in figure 3-5 is then measured off at the midpoint between the bow and the stern. Using a 1-inch by 1-inch batten, nails are set in the top sideboards so that the batten will lie on the intersection of the top line with the bow line and stern line. The center of the batten is then pulled down to the 2-inch sheer mark, and the batten is tacked in place. The smooth,

3-6. Marking the angle of the bow. This angle can be measured but is usually marked off by eye.

curved sheer line is then drawn using the batten as a marking edge. Using a similar process, the "smooth curve cut" on the bottom sideboards is then marked.

Using a power handsaw, the bow and the stern angles are cut with the boards still paired (figure 3-7).Then both the sheer and bottom lines are cut (figure 3-8). Before proceeding further, these edges must be smoothed up with a plane.

3-7. Cutting the angle of the stern or transom on the paired bottom sideboards.

3-8. *Cutting the sheer line with a hand power saw.*

Before disassembling the pairs of boards, the boards are marked for cutting the lap bevels as shown in figures 3-9 and 3-10. The best tool for this marking job is a small carpenter's trysquare (figure 3-11).

When the bevels are marked, the pairs of boards are disassembled, and the portion to be removed is rough cut using a very sharp drawshave (figure 3-12). It is possible to cut these bevels on a table saw or radial-arm saw, but the preparation required, the extreme care that must be taken during the sawing operation, and the requirement for one or two extra pairs of hands during the cut make using a drawshave more practical for the lone builder. When the board has been worked down with the drawshave to the approximate dimensions of the bevel, the remainder of the bevel is cut with a regular carpenter's plane (figure 3-13). At the end of each board, it is necessary to feather the last two to three inches of the bevel down to a knife edge rather than leaving the ⅛-inch square portion shown in figure 3-9. If this is not done, a gap will result where the sideboards meet both the stem and the transom, and the skiff will leak if water attains this level.

An inner stem of red oak must be cut to the dimensions shown in figure 3-14, using a table saw (figure 3-15) or a radial-arm saw. Once the stem is sawed out and smoothed with a plane, the skiff is ready to be "set up".

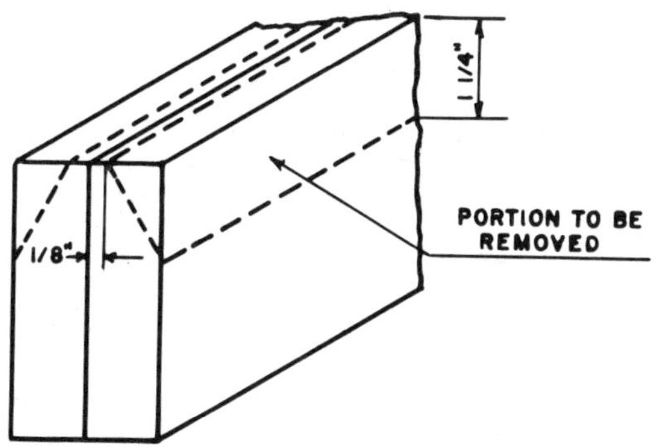

3-9. Paired sideboards with the bevel marked for cutting.

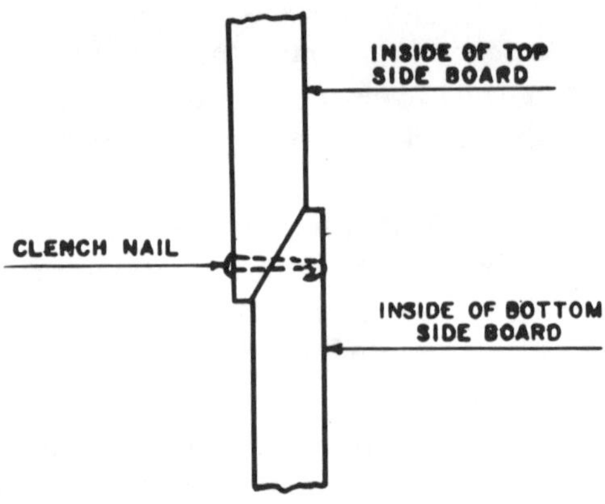

3-10. The joint between the top and bottom sideboards.

3-11. Using a trysquare to mark the bevel for the joint between the top and bottom sideboards.

3-12. *Roughing out the bevel with a drawshave.*

3-13. *Planing the bevel to the finish dimension.*

3-14. The inner stem.

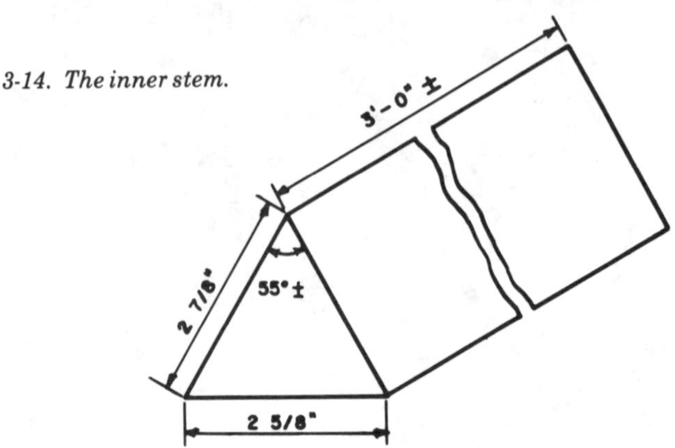

3-15. Cutting the stem on a table saw.

ſetting Up the ſkiff

Before further construction can proceed, a bending mold must be built as shown in figure 4-1. This need not be made of finish lumber, but good stock at least 1-inch thick should be used, since the mold will receive considerable strain as the skiff is bent into shape. Care should also be taken that the mold is symmetrical about a vertical centerline, since to a great extent the mold will determine the final shape of the boat.

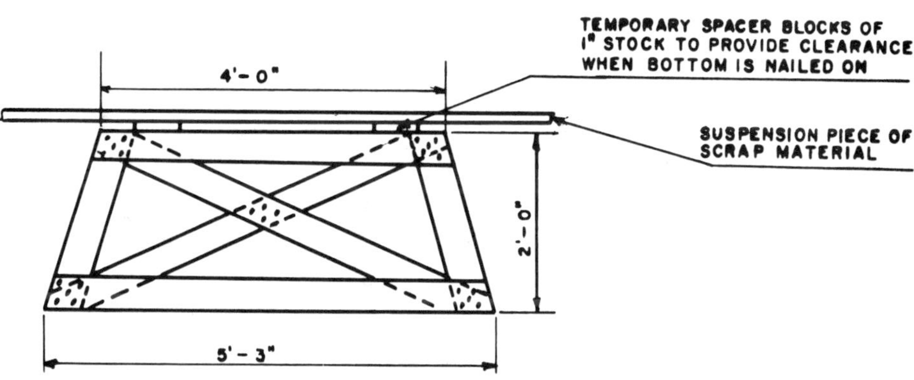

4-1. The bending mold.

After the mold has been built, the bottom sideboards or planks are nailed to the inner stem, with the bevel toward the floor as shown in figure 4-2. Take care that both sideboards are nailed to the stem at exactly the same point and that the forward edges of the sideboards are exactly in contact with the apex of the triangular inner stem. The sideboards should be nailed to the stem with 8-penny nails, which should be driven below the surface with a large nail set (figures 4-3 and 4-4). Obviously, extreme stress will develop at this nail joint as the sides are bent into their final position. To overcome this, scraps of wood, trapezoidal in cross-section, are temporarily nailed to each side of the bow, and C-clamps are tightened on the scraps (figure 4-5).

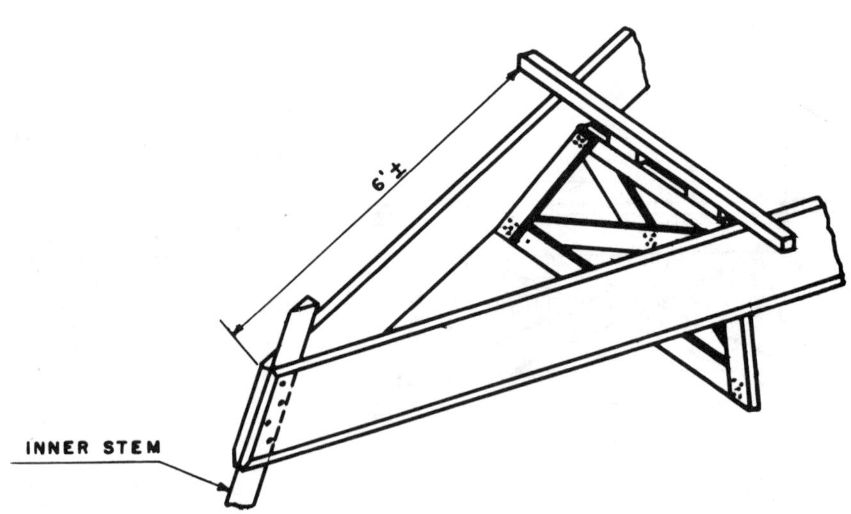

4-2. *The bottom sideboards nailed to the stem, and the mold suspended in place.*

4-3. *Nailing the first bottom sideboard to the stem.*

4-4. *Nailing the second bottom sideboard to the stem.*

4-5. *Clamps in place at the stem to keep things in place while the sides are bent to shape.*

Now, marks are made on each sideboard approximately six feet back from the bow, and the bending mold is inserted between the sideboards as shown in figures 4-2 and 4-6. Bending pieces, detailed in figure 4-7, are then fastened to each bottom sideboard by using C-clamps (figure 4-8). A rope is threaded through holes drilled in the ends of the bending pieces, and it is hauled taut and tied off. By tightening this rope, the bottom sideboards are brought to approximately their final position in a series of bending steps (figure 4-9). Auxiliary bending pieces, detailed in figure 4-10, are then clamped to the bottom sideboards close to the bending mold (figure 4-11). By tightening the rope shown in figure 4-10, the sideboards are brought into close contact with the bending mold. Both bottom sideboards are then temporarily nailed to the mold (figure 4-12).

4-6. Setting the bending mold in place approximately six feet aft of the stem.

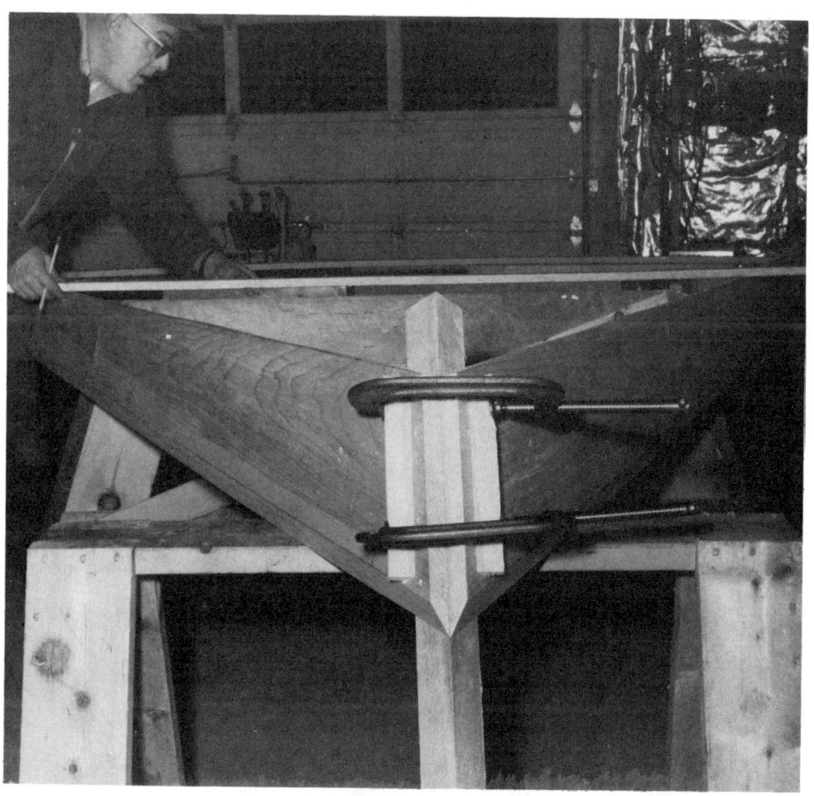

4-7. The bending pieces used at the stern.

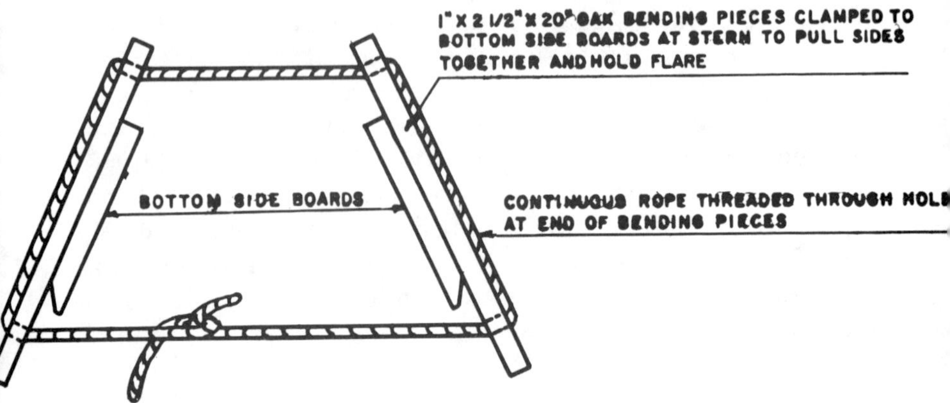

4-8. Clamping the bending pieces to the after ends of the bottom sideboards.

4-9. The bottom sideboards bent around approximately to their final positions.

4-10. The auxiliary bending pieces at the mold.

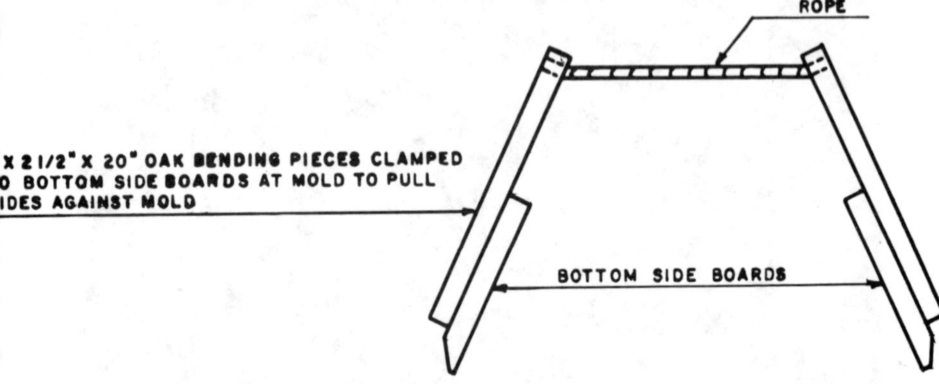

4-11. The auxiliary bending pieces clamped to the bottom sideboards to pull them against the flare of the mold.

4-12. Temporarily nailing the sides to the mold.

With the sideboards in approximately their final location, a temporary board is nailed across the after ends of the sideboards at the location of the transom or stern board (figures 4-13 and 4-14). By using a carpenter's bevel against this temporary board, both the flare and the angle of the transom can be determined, and a transom board can be cut as detailed in figure 4-15. Approximate dimensions of a transom board are shown in figure 4-15; but again, these can be modified to fit the builder's wishes. The bottom of the transom board can be prebevelled on a table saw, but considerable care should be exercised in cutting the compound bevel at the sides of the transom. It is best to do this with a regular carpenter's handsaw. Once cut, the transom is fastened in place with 8-penny nails (figure 4-16).

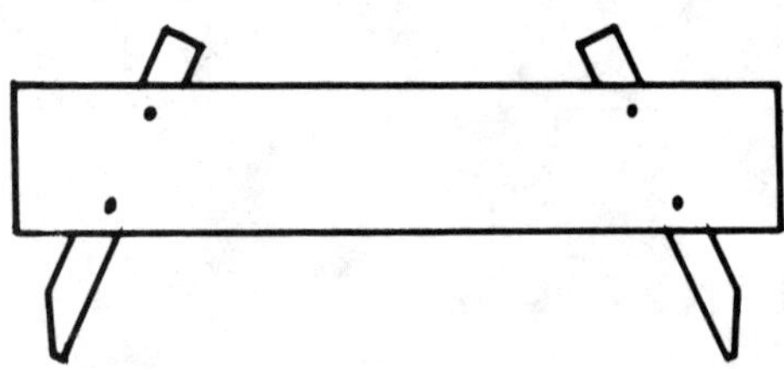

4-13. Temporary board nailed to the after ends of the bottom sideboards for measuring and equalizing the compound bevel.

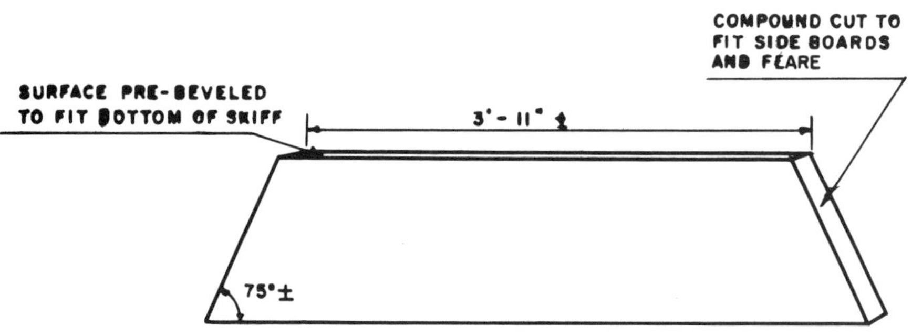

4-14. *Nailing a temporary board to the after end of the bottom sideboards.*

4-15. *Approximate dimensions of the bottom of the sternboard or transom.*

4-16. *Nailing the bottom section of the transom in place.*

The skiff is trued up by nailing a temporary brace of scrape lumber from the stern to a wall of the shop (figure 4-17). The bow is similarly braced. A nylon line is stretched from the stem to the center of the transom. The skiff is then brought into perfect symmetry by taking a series of measurements while bracing, cross bracing, and warping the two sides into final position (figures 4-18 and 4-19). Final cross bracing is then added to keep the assembly rigid (figure 4-20), and the skiff is ready to have its bottom applied.

4-17. Nailing a temporary brace at the stern for alignment purposes to make both sides of the skiff true.

4-18. *Measurements randomly taken on each side of the centerline string must be equal before the bottom is cross-braced.*

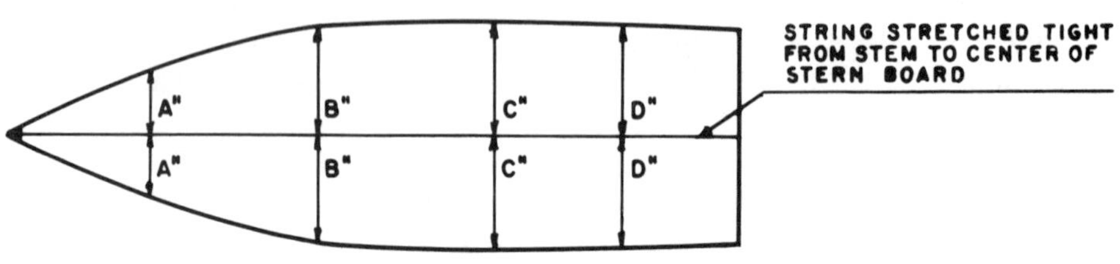

4-19. *Measuring against the centerline string to determine symmetry before nailing down the temporary middle brace.*

4-20. *The skiff braced and ready for the bottom planking.*

5.

Planking the Bottom

Before the bottom can be planked it is first necessary to bevel the bottom of the sideboards or planks as shown in figure 5-1. This is ordinarily done by working the bevel for two or three feet at both the bow and the stern rather than trying to do the entire length of the sideboards at once, since the addition of a few bottom planks or boards at each end of the skiff will greatly stiffen the structure and insure that the symmetry is not disturbed. The initial cuts for this bevel can be done with a drawshave (figure 5-2). Extreme care should be exercised, however, to preclude cutting below the inside corner of the bottom boards (figure 5-1) or the uniformity of the bottom will be destroyed. The bevel can be finished in most locations with a plane (figure 5-3) or with a good, sharp spokeshave. During this process, the bevel of both sideboards should be constantly checked with a straightedge several inches wide to insure a close fit of the bottom boards (figure 5-4). Twisted cotton caulking is placed along the bottom of the transom and the bottom of the sideboards, which will then be ready to accept the first stern plank (figure 5-5). Twisted cotton caulking is now difficult to obtain, so if it cannot be found, untwisted cotton caulking can be used by twisting it by hand.

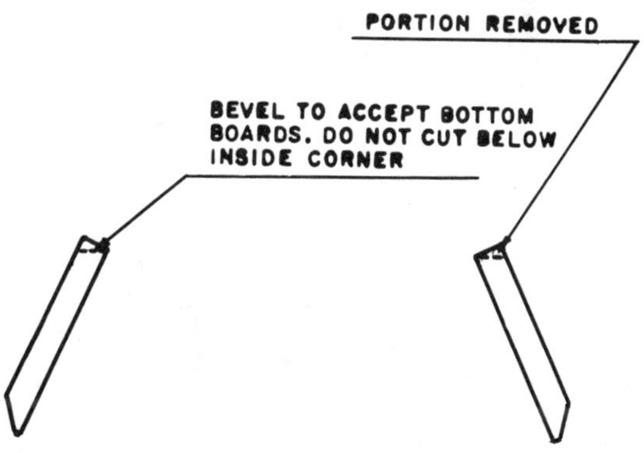

5-1. The bevel on the bottom of the sideboards.

5-2. *Using a drawshave to bevel the sides to accept the bottom planking.*

5-3. *Finishing the bevel of the sideboards with a plane.*

5-4. *Using a straightedge to check the bevel of the sideboards.*

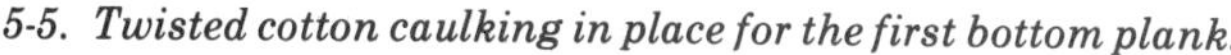

5-5. *Twisted cotton caulking in place for the first bottom plank.*

Before being nailed in place, each bottom board must be bevelled on one edge as shown in figure 5-6 and 5-7. If this is not done, there will be no room for the expansion of the wood when the bottom boards swell after the skiff is launched. The bottom of the skiff will literally swell away from the sideboards, producing a leaking boat. After the first board is properly bevelled, it is nailed in place (figure 5-8). Each plank should be cut a little longer than necessary, then after it has been fastened down it should be sawed to the exact contour of the side of the skiff by holding a handsaw against the skiff side as shown in figure 5-15. The end of each plank is planed with a block plane and given a final sandpapering to insure that the bottom board exactly fits the contour of the sideboards.

5-6. Cross-section of the bottom planking. One edge of each plank is beveled to take the caulking and to prevent the bottom from swelling off.

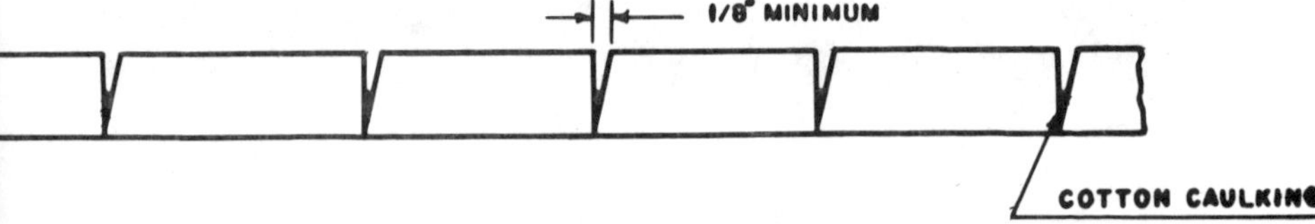

5-7. Using a bench stop while a caulking bevel is cut on one edge of a bottom plank.

5-8. *Nailing the first bottom plank in place.*

After a few planks have been installed at the stern end of the skiff, the sideboards are bevelled at the bow. In the area of the stem it will be necessary to work the bevel with a chisel. Once this bevel has been cut, the inner stem is sawed off flush with the beveled sides (figure 5-9), and the entire bow assembly is planed smooth (figure 5-10). Then another foot or so of bevel is cut, again using a drawshave, plane, or spokeshave.

5-9. *Sawing the stem off flush with the sides after the bevel has been cut on the sideboards.*

5-10. *Planing the stem and sideboard bevels to accept the bottom boards.*

The bow plank is not notched to fit the angle of the sideboards at the bow; rather it bridges this angle (figure 5-11). This produces a somewhat tricky cut when preparing the false stem, which will be described later, but it does add strength to the bow plank. Since the bow plank is relatively small, it is drilled before fastening to prevent splitting (figure 5-12). Once drilled, it is nailed in place (figure 5-13), and, as with all the other bottom planks, the nails are well set (figure 5-14). Figures 5-15, 5-16, and 5-17 show the bow plank being trimmed, planed, and sandpapered.

Bottom planks are added a few at a time, alternating from the bow to the stern (figure 5-18). Bracing and cross bracing is removed as encountered, until eventually there is only one more plank to go (figure 5-19). The final plank ordinarily will not have parallel sides but will have to be cut somewhat trapezoidal in shape to fit the opening left for it.

Once the final plank is in place, the skiff is turned rightside up for the first time (figure 5-20), ready for the next step in construction, that of adding the top sideboards.

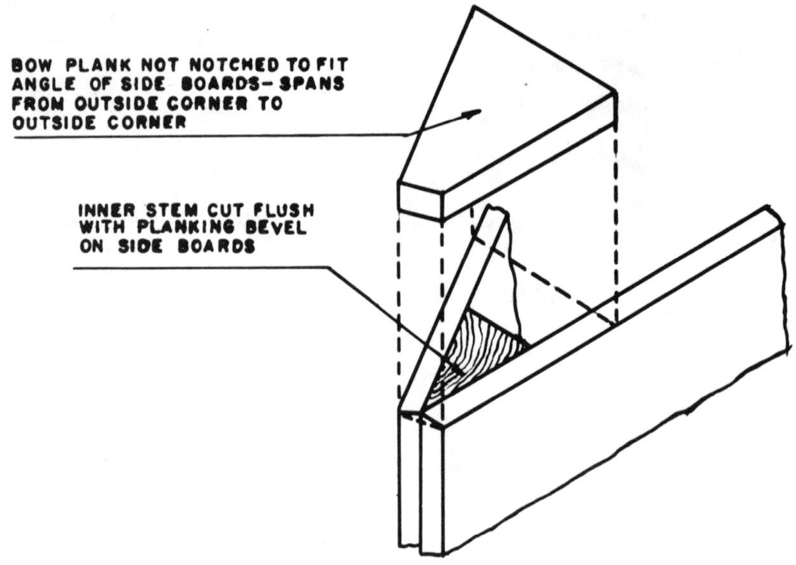

5-11. Detail of the bow area.

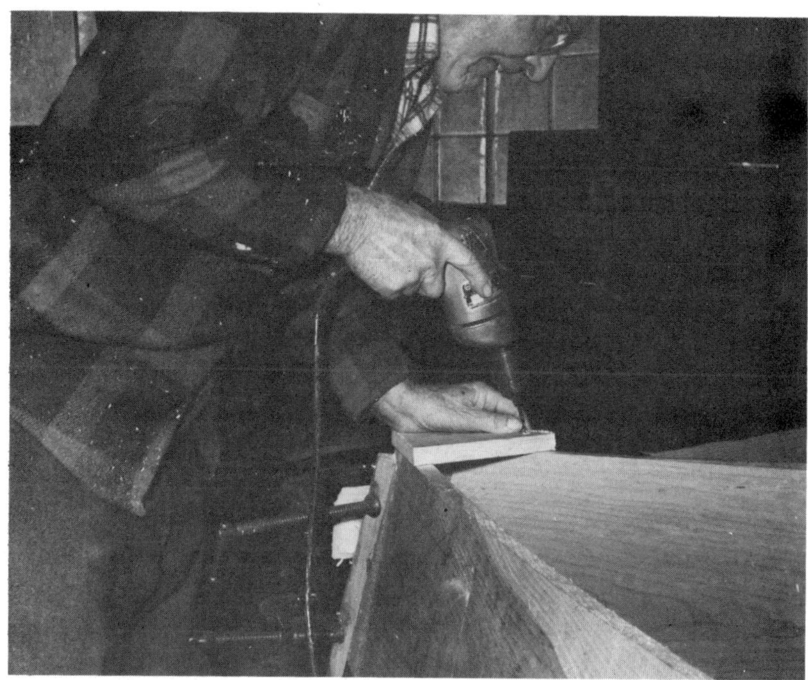

5-12. Drilling for the fastenings of the forward bottom plank to avoid splitting when the fastenings are driven.

5-13. Nailing the forward bottom plank in place.

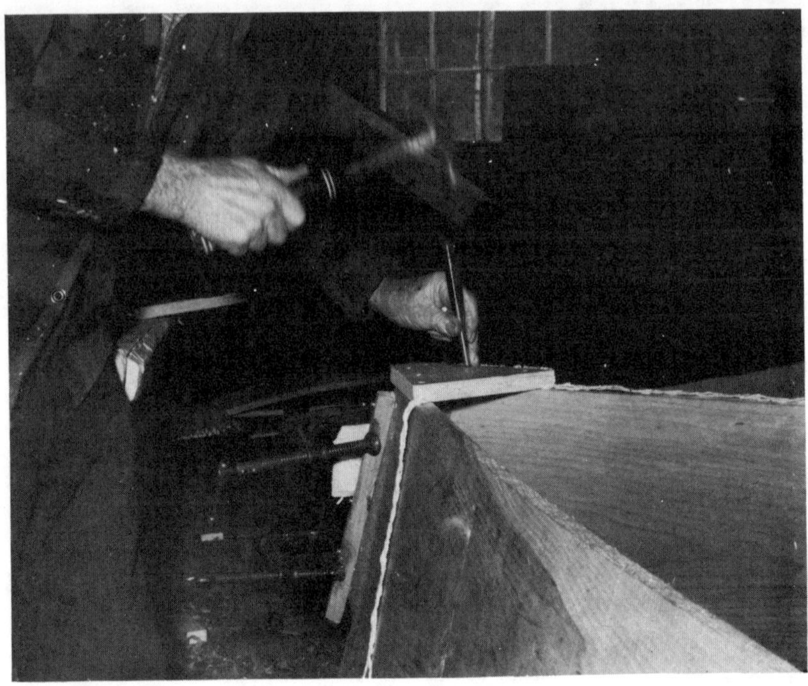

5-14. *Setting the nails in the forward bottom plank.*

5-15. *Sawing off the forward bottom plank to fit the contour of the skiff's sides.*

5-16. Planing the edge of the forward bottom plank.

5-17. Final sandpapering of the forward bottom plank to insure a close fit to the contour of the sides.

5-18. Bottom planking is installed at each end of the skiff to provide stability before the middle cross-bracing is removed.

5-19. One plank to go.

5-20. *The skiff turned rightside-up.*

6

Adding the Top Sideboards

Only one step, fastening the side cleats in position, remains before the top sideboards or planks can be added. The side cleats are detailed in figure 6-1 and their locations are shown in figure 6-2. Although figure 6-1 shows a side cleat finished and in position, the top should not be actually cut off until the sides are in place. The cleats should be cut sufficiently long to extend above the top sideboards at this point in the construction. The bevel on the cleats where they meet the bottom of the skiff should be cut before installation. This can be done on a table saw with the saw bevel set at 45 degrees. The cleats fixed closely together, shown with the six-inch spacing (on center) in figure 6-2, will become the final location of the center and forward seats. Again, the dimensions shown are not firm, and if a different location of seats is desired, the spacing can be modified. Obviously this would be done for a longer skiff.

6-1. Side cleat detail.

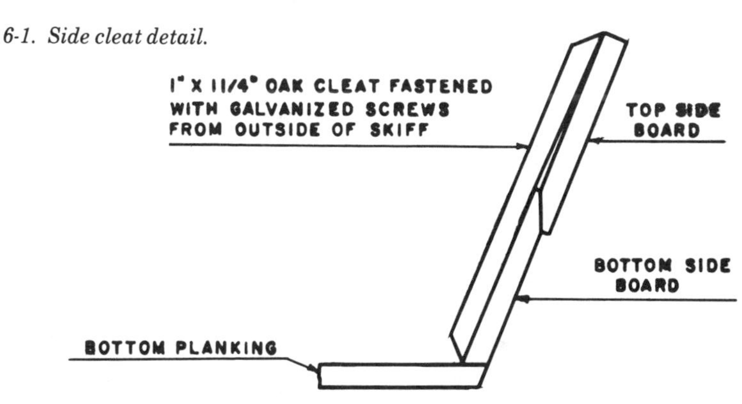

6-2. The location of the side cleats.

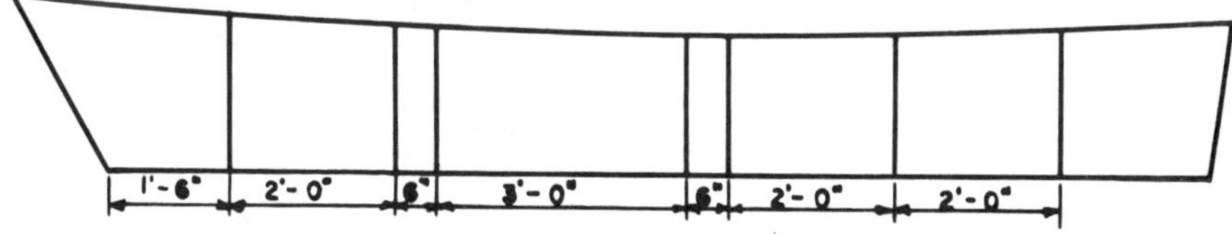

The upright cleats as they are installed are temporarily held in position with C-clamps (figure 6-3), and the sides and cleats are drilled before being fastened from the outside with galvanized screws (figure 6-4). The corner cleats that fit where the sides meet the transom (figure 6-5) are also installed at this time. The necessary bevels are measured with a carpenter's bevel and the cleats are planed to insure a tight fit (figure 6-6). They are fastened in the same manner as the side cleats, except they are also fastened through from the outside of the transom.

6-3. *Side cleats being screwed in place.*

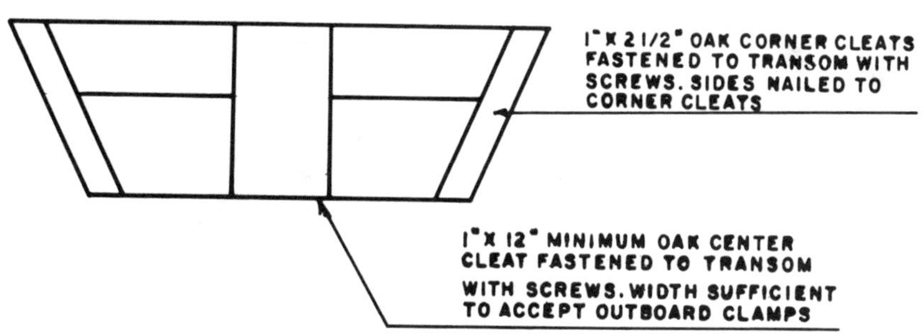

6-4. *Another look at the side cleats as they are screwed in place.*

6-5. *Reinforcing cleats on the sternboard or transom.*

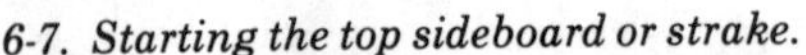

6-6. *Corner cleats being planed and fitted.*

6-7. *Starting the top sideboard or strake.*

The next step is to install the top sideboards. Each board is placed in position and fastened to the stem with eight-penny nails (figure 6-7). They are then worked into their final position by working your way aft, clamping as you go and nailing through the lap joint at short intervals. As soon as a short section of the top sideboard is clamped in its final position, the lap joint is drilled to receive the clench nails (figure 6-8). Clench nails are driven from the outside (figure 6-9) and are always backed up with a clenching iron (figure 6-10). These nails are also staggered so that alternate nails are close to opposite edges of the lap joint to insure a water-tight joint. As mentioned earlier, special rivets can be used to fasten the lap joint if clench nails are not available, but this ordinarily will require a two-man operation due to the special tools required for their use.

6-8. Drilling for the clench nails at the lap joint between the top and bottom sideboard.

6-9. *Driving clench nails.*

6-10. *Using a clenching iron to back up the clench nails as they are driven.*

7

Finishing the Inside of the Skiff

Although at this point the skiff has taken its final form, a multitude of cutting and fitting jobs remain to be done to finish the inside of the vessel. These will be described in their normal order of completion.

The middle and forward seats are installed as follows: Seat supports, shown in figure 7-1, are nailed in place on the side cleats installed for this purpose. The supports are cut from pine, and all outside edges are slightly bevelled with a plane. The supports are installed so that the finished seat height will be approximately 10 inches above the bottom of the skiff (figure 7-2).

A reinforcing piece for each interior seat is also installed (figures 7-3 and 7-4). This is a tricky piece to cut, since it involves compound cuts at each end to fit both the flare and the angle of the sides. Here again, the carpenter's bevel comes into its prime as does the hand saw and block plane. On small skiffs where the span of the seat is not long, this piece can be omitted, but for strength and durability of the seat in larger skiffs it is recommended. After being cut and fitted, the reinforcing piece is attached to the seat support.

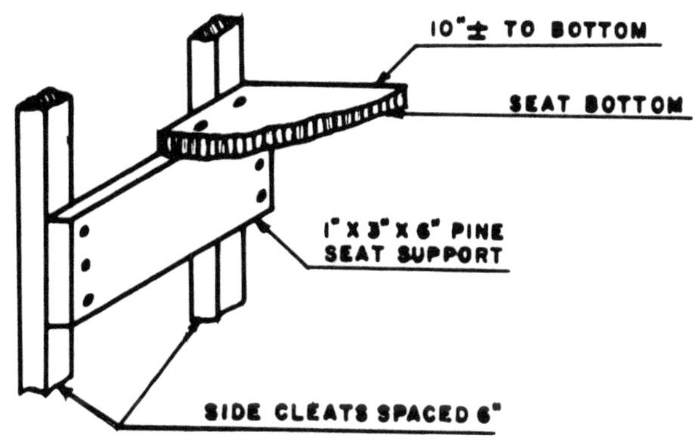

7-1. Middle and forward seat support detail.

7-2. *Installing the horizontal cleat for the middle seat.*

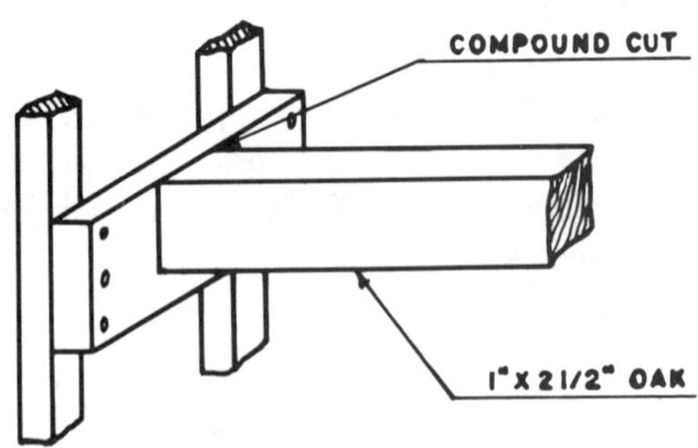

7-3. *The reinforcing piece for the middle and forward seats.*

The seat board itself also requires compound cuts on either end. After being cut and fitted, it is fastened to the seat supports (figure 7-1) and also to the reinforcing piece spanning the skiff. The top edges of the seat should be bevelled with a plane, and the corners should be somewhat rounded with a chisel where the seat meets the upright cleats. The final installation of the middle seat is shown in figure 7-5.

7-4. *Fastening the reinforcing piece for the middle seat in place.*

7-5. *The middle seat in position.*

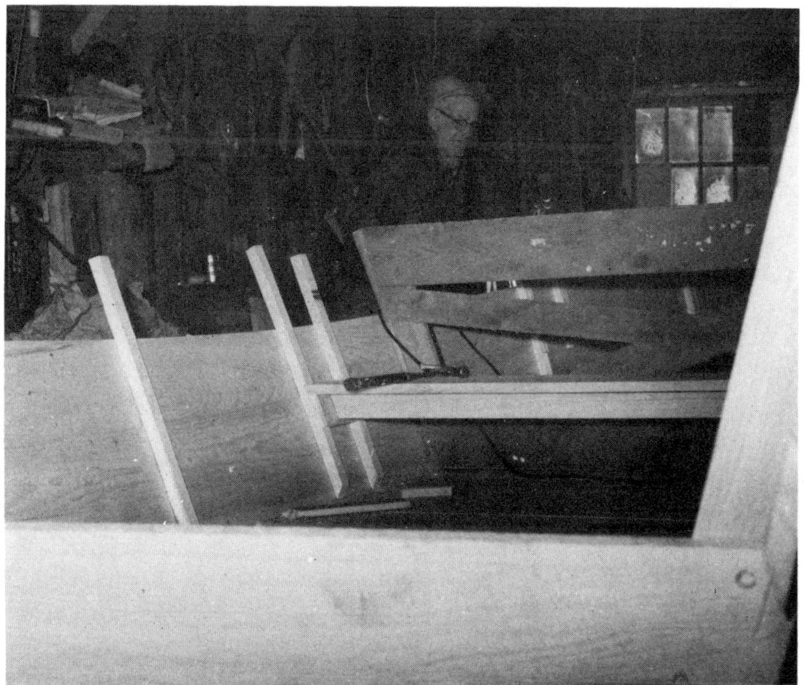

As soon as the middle and forward seats are installed to maintain the stability of the sides, the bending mold can be removed, and the installation of the 1-inch by 6-inch oak inner clamp or keelson can be started (figure 7-6). The inner clamp is first "worked" into the boat under both seats, and the forward end is marked and cut to fit snugly in the bow. The forward end is bevelled to provide a good joint at the inner stem. As soon as the forward end of the inner clamp is fitted, the stern end is cut off to permit the clamp to lie flat on the bottom of the skiff. A tight fit at the transom is not necessary, but the clamp should not be cut so short that the stern center cleat, detailed in figure 6-5, will not cover the joint.

7-6. *The mold has been removed and the inner clamp or keelson, which goes along the bottom, is being fitted.*

7-7. *The center upright cleat is in position for marking the after end of the inner clamp for final cutting.*

7-8. *Clamp detail.*

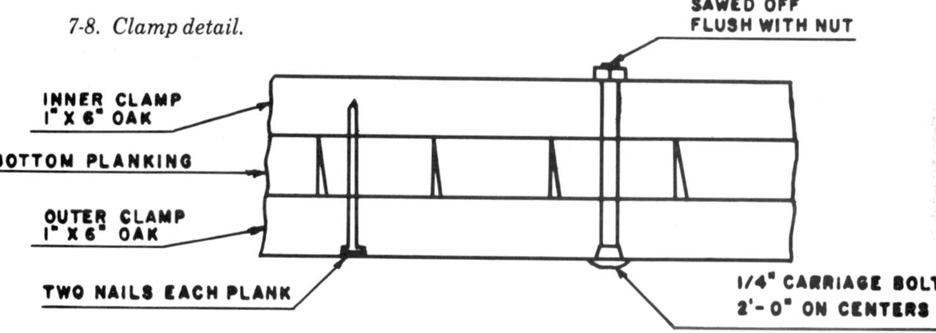

With the inner clamp in place but not fastened down, the stern center cleat is then located at the center of the transom (figure 7-7) and is used to mark the final cut at the after end of the inner clamp. The clamp is removed, and the angle of the transom is marked on it using a carpenter's bevel. The inner clamp is cut off to the correct angle, repositioned on the bottom of the skiff in its final location, and temporarily fastened to the bottom of the skiff. (Figure 7-8 shows a detail of the inner clamp, bottom plank, outer clamp or keel, and final fastenings, the installation of which will be described later.) The stern center cleat is then placed between the end of the inner clamp and the transom, and fastened in place by screwing through the transom from the outside.

A knee of 2-inch oak is cut on a band saw and fastened in place between the clamp and the center stern cleat (figures 7-9 and 7-10). This knee may be fastened by nailing or screwing through the transom, but if extra strength is desired as is necessary if the boat will be used with a relatively high horsepower motor, it should have added fastenings in the form of carriage bolts. The carriage bolt going through the transom inner clamp and knee can be installed at this point, but the carriage bolt through the bottom should await the addition of the outer clamp or keel.

The stern seat supports are installed next (figure 7-11). They are fastened in place by drilling and nailing with clench nails (figure 7-12 and 7-13). The stern seat is then cut, fitted, and fastened (figures 7-11 and 7-14). Fastening here is limited to nails driven down into the seat supports. It should be noted that the stern seat is not fitted around the corner and center cleats. This leaves a space for water to drain off the seat and allows room to attach a safety chain for the outboard.

Using much the same process as was used for the bottom transom board, the top transom board is measured, cut with the necessary compound angles, and installed. Again, fastening is with screws from the outside of the transom through to the center and corner cleats (figure 7-15). Once these screws have been installed, the top sideboards are nailed to the top of the transom in the same fashion as the bottom sideboards.

7-9. Stern knee detail.

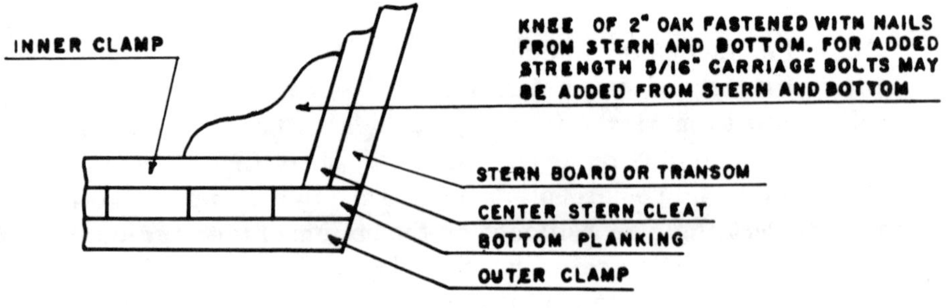

7-10. *The stern knee in place and fastened.*

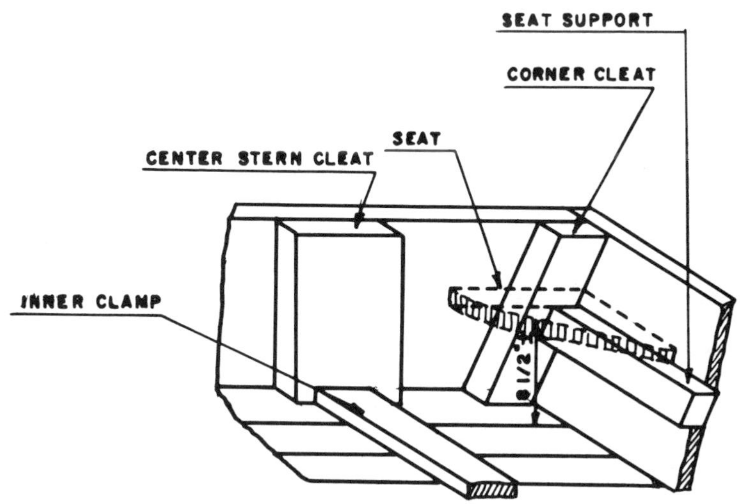

7-11. *Stern seat detail (stern knee is not shown).*

7-12. *Drilling the horizontal cleat for the stern seat prior to fastening it in place with clench nails.*

7-13 *Using a clenching iron to fasten the horizontal cleat for the stern seat in place.*

7-14. *The stern seat has been fitted and is being fastened in place.*

7-15. *Fastening the top of the sternboard or transom in place.*

The joint between the upper and lower sections of the transom may tend to open up, since the oak used in this construction is usually obtained unseasoned. This problem can be overcome to a degree by inserting a strip of pine about ½-inch thick between the bottom and the top portions of the transom. Perhaps an easier method is to let the joint open during the first year of use and fill it with epoxy or polyester putty before the skiff is painted for its second season.

Now is the time for all the cleats to be sawed off to their final height. The stern cleats are sawed with a relatively shallow bevel (figure 7-16). The upright side cleats can be sawed at a 45-degree angle to match their bottom bevel, or they can be cut by eye without detracting from the finished appearance of the vessel. (In the skiff shown under construction here, the side cleats were cut off after the gunwale scrub strips were installed—see figure 8-3.)

7-16. Sawing the upright center cleat flush with the top of the transom.

The false stem is next prepared (figure 7-17 and 7-18). Again, this is an extremely tricky cut that can be made on a table saw. However, specific dimensional details cannot be given, since each skiff will end up with slightly different angles. It is largely a matter of cutting and fitting. After the false stem has been fitted to fair roughly into the sides of the skiff, bedding compound is applied to the joint, and the false stem is drilled and nailed in place (figure 7-19). Final shaping of the false stem to insure a perfect match with the sides of the skiff is accomplished with a plane and scraper (figure 7-20). Details on how to make such a scraper can be found in my book *How to Build Bamboo Fly Rods* published by Winchester Press.

One more difficult compound cut remains—that of the breasthook (figure 7-21 and 7-22). If possible this should be made of pine somewhat thicker than that used for the sides of the boat, possibly up to 1¼ inches in finished thickness. The exact dimensions of the breasthook cannot be predicted; it is again a matter of cutting and fitting. As with the forward bottom plank, the breasthook is relatively small. It, too, should be drilled before being nailed in place to prevent splitting.

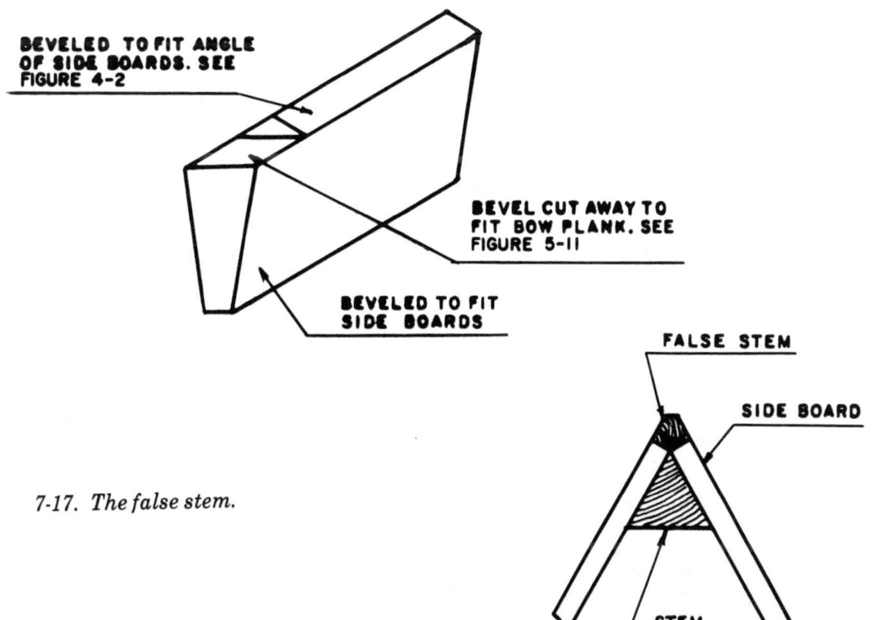

7-17. *The false stem.*

7-18. *The bow ready for the installation of the false stem. Note that the bottom plank is cut squarely across and is flush with the forward edges of the sideboards.*

7-19. *The false stem being fastened in place. Note the bedding compound used in the joint.*

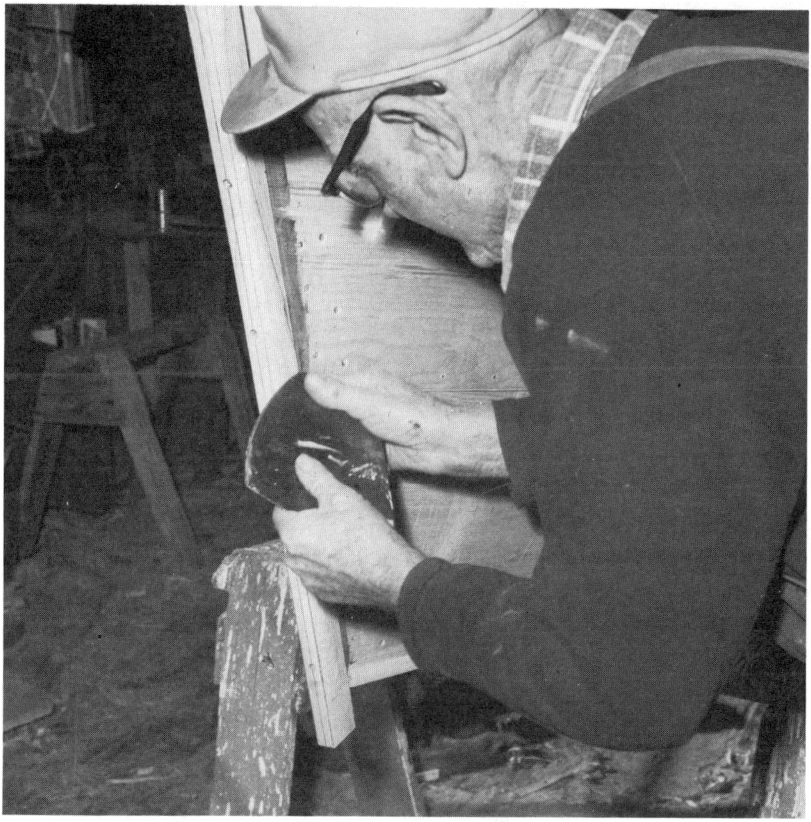

7-20. *Working the false stem down with a scraper to match exactly the contour of the sides.*

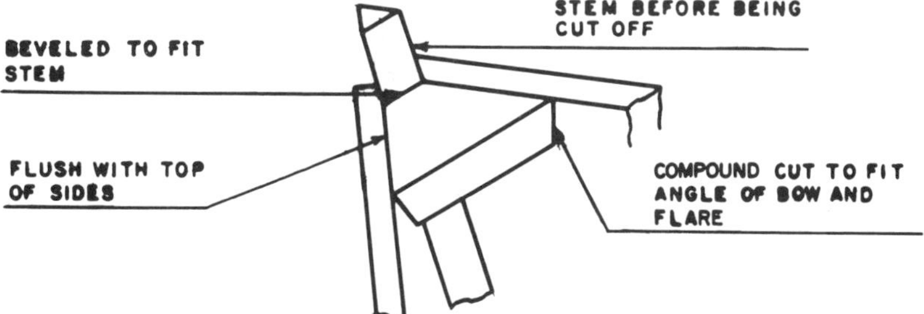

7-21. *The breasthook.*

7-22. *Fitting the breasthook.*

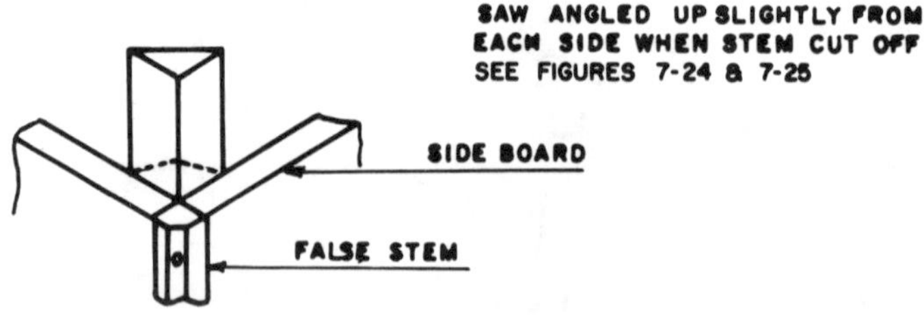

7-23. *Detail of the bow.*

7-24. *Sawing off the stem.*

7-25. *The finished bow section.*

8

Finishing the Skiff

Gunwale scrub strips as shown in figure 8-1 are installed on both sides of the skiff as a final step before the boat is again turned bottom up. If the skiff is to be used for play, the scrub strips can be of pine; if to be used for work, the strips should be of oak for durability. In either case, the strips are worked into position by aligning short sections flush with the top sideboards or planks and clamping them in place (figure 8-2). Once properly aligned, they are fastened by driving screws through the scrub strip into the top sideboard, and the tops of the side cleats are sawed off flush with the gunwale (figure 8-3).

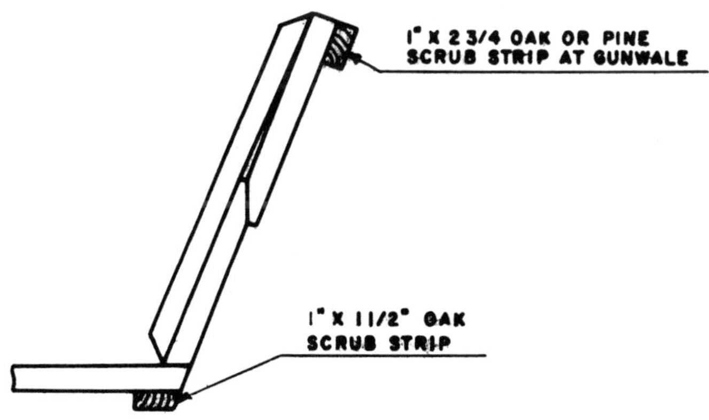

8-1. The scrub or rubbing strips.

8-2. *The gunwale scrub strip clamped in place, ready for fastening.*

8-3. Sawing off the side cleats.

The skiff is now turned bottom up so the bottom seams can be caulked (figure 8-4). Cotton caulking is worked into each seam in the bottom planking with a caulking iron to start the strands (figure 8-5), and a special caulking roller is used to fill the remainder of the seams (figure 8-6). The proper placement of the caulking in the seams is shown in figure 5-6, and the special caulking roller, which can be made in a home shop, is shown in figure 8-7.

8-4. *The skiff upside-down, ready for the bottom seams to be caulked.*

8-5. Using a caulking iron to start a strand of twisted cotton caulking.

8-6. Using a caulking roller to roll the cotton into the seams.

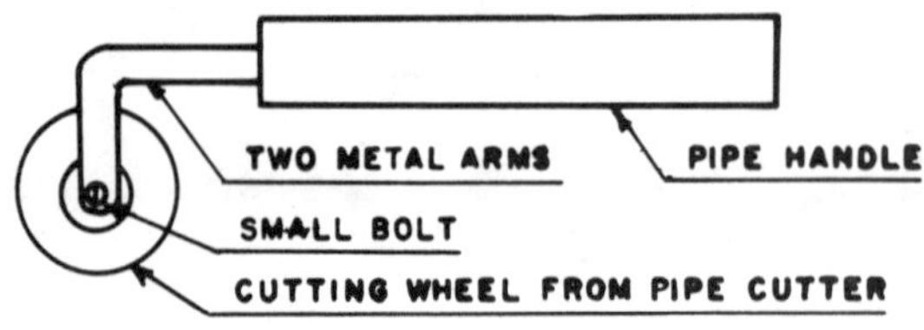

8-7. A homemade caulking roller.

If the boat is to be used in salt water, the next step is to apply a coat of antifouling paint to the bottom (figure 8-8). In fresh water this may not be imperative. But if antifouling paint is to be used, it should be applied now, before the bottom scrub strips are fitted, so full protection against marine growth and organisms will be afforded the bottom planking under the scrub strips.

8-8. Painting the bottom with antifouling paint before the bottom strips are installed.

Once the antifouling paint is on, a 1-inch-by-6-inch oak outer clamp or keel is positioned and nailed in place (figure 8-9). Details of the fastening are shown in figure 7-8. Two nails are driven through each plank in a staggered pattern so that the nails actually penetrate to the inner clamp of 1-inch-by-6-inch oak. One-quarter-inch carriage bolts are then installed on two-foot centers, the entire length of the outer clamp, making sure that none of the holes bored for the carriage bolts are located near the edge of a bottom plank. The carriage bolts must extend through the outer clamp, the planking, and the inner clamp and are tightened securely on a flat washer to give added strength to the bottom of the skiff. Holes for the carriage bolts should not be oversized, but should be exactly ¼-inch for a ¼-inch bolt. This will necessitate driving the bolts through the assembly (figure 8-10).

8-9. Nailing the outside center clamp or keel in place.

8-10. *Driving bolts through the outer and inner clamps.*

When the fastening is completed, the forward end of the outer clamp strip is trimmed to conform with the sides of the skiff (figure 8-11), and 1-inch-by-1½-inch oak scrub strips are nailed along each side of the bottom (figures 8-1 and 8-12).

At this point the only remaining construction is the installation of oarlocks, which is done after the skiff is again turned right-side up. If desired, thole pins, shown in figure 8-13, can be used in lieu of oarlocks. The thole-pin blocks are fastened to the sides of the skiff by driving screws through from the outside planking.

Now the skiff can be painted and puttied. The correct procedure is to paint the skiff, putty all nail and screw holes, and then apply a second coat of paint. Marine seam compound should be used for putty, and this compound should be bought in a color that will approximate the paint color being used.

8-11. Trimming the forward end of the outside clamp.

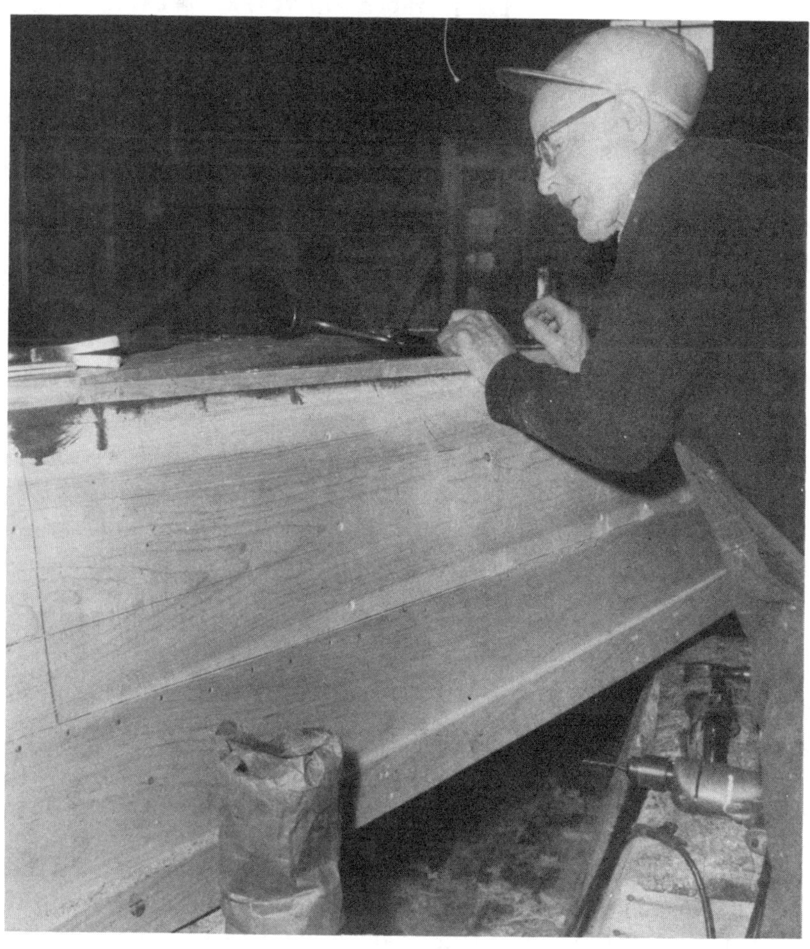

8-12. *Fastening the bottom scrub strips in place.*

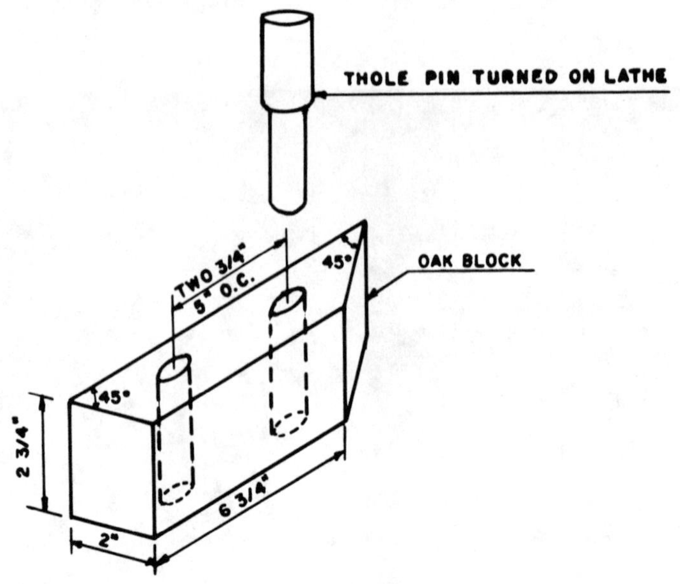

8-13. *Thole pins, a time-honored substitute for oar locks.*

There are a few tricks to painting the skiff. If the bottom is painted before the installation of the scrub strips, the scrub strips should be given a prime coat of paint before they are puttied. A second coat of antifouling paint should then be applied, but to prevent antifouling paint from running on the sides of the skiff, do not paint the area between the bottom and the waterline until the boat is turned over. The area between the waterline and the top of the sideboards, however, is painted while the skiff is upsidedown, since this will prevent the lighter-colored paint from running down into the antifouling paint.

Once these portions of the outside of the skiff have been given two coats of paint, the skiff is again turned upright, and the remainder of the antifouling paint can be applied between the waterline and the bottom of the skiff. Then two coats of marine enamel are applied to the interior of the skiff. The boring of holes at the bow to receive a "painter" or bow line completes the finishing process (figure 8-14). The vessel is ready for launching.

My father was once asked how long it took to build a skiff. His response was, "A week. I suppose if you went at it hammer and tong, you might do it in less than a week, but I doubt it like hell!" Your first venture in building a skiff may well take more than a 40-hour week, but the results are well worth the effort.

8-14. *The downeast skiff painted and ready for launching.*

Index